Am I Talking To Somebody?

From My Heart To Yours
Father Claude Scrima OFM
His Story and The Love He Inspires

Written and Compiled by
Margaret Fucillo

Copyright © 2024, Margaret Fucillo

ALL RIGHTS RESERVED.
No part of this publication may be reproduced, stored in a retrieval system or transmitted in any form or by any means whatsoever, whether electronic, mechanical, magnetic recording, or photocopying, without the prior written approval of the Copyright holder or Publisher, excepting brief quotations for inclusion in book reviews.

Published by:

Janaway Publishing, Inc.
Santa Maria, California 93454
(805) 925-1952
www.janawaygenealogy.com

2024

ISBN: 978-1-59641-484-6

Made in the United States of America

DEDICATION:

All North Enders dedicate this book to you, Father Claude. We love you for your wisdom, dedication, humility, kindness, intellect, love for all people, your generosity, compassion and devotion to helping all those in need.

ACKNOWLEDGMENTS:

Thank you to all who contributed to this book. Many thanks to Doreen Merola for the title: Am I Talking to Somebody? Also, to Andy Gaus for all his help. Finally, thank you to the Scrima family for your stories, pictures and most importantly your infinite love for Uncle Claude.

Table of Contents

Introduction viii

1 The Beginning 1
2 School and Beyond, Becoming a Priest 7
3 Father Claude's Contributions to the North End
   and the Franciscans 15
4 The Terrible Fall 21
5 North Enders and Friends, Fond Memories and
   Tributes 27
6 Father Claude: Families' Stories 37
7 My Connection to Father Claude 49
Pictures: Parishioners/Friends 60
Pictures: Clergy 64

INTRODUCTION:

I had returned to my roots in the North End on a more regular basis. I joined some committees and organizations and I attend the Italian Mass at St. Leonard's Church. One Sunday, I met Father Claude at the entrance of the church as he welcomed people inside for Mass. He asked me my name and I told him. He then replied, "You look like a Kelly!" I pointed to Fleet Street, which is perpendicular to Hanover Street (almost across the street from the church) and countered with, "No, Father, I am really from Fleet Street and a Fucillo ~ I do tend to color my hair blonde or red sometimes just to throw you off!"

I developed a strong connection with Father Claude from the first time I personally interacted with him. He led me on a treasure hunt to find the statues that lined the walls of Saint Anthony's Church (the "Lower Church" that has since been turned into Saint Joseph's Hall) and the Grotto, which was situated at the back of the Lower Church. I was especially interested in finding the Pieta, the statue that stood at the center of the Grotto and welcomed all who entered. He proceeded to take me on a journey into my past, my grandmother's sanctuary where she spent most of her time attending Mass, with me at her side. My friendship with Father Claude began as a very mystical journey, and one that continues until present times.

How did I begin to love this man? First of all, it was immediate. He radiated an inner peace; he was friendly and eager to chat to all he met while walking the streets of the North End. I think he knew almost everyone, and everyone knew and loved him. Most of all he was a humble man whose life's mission was to help people. I felt I was home.

His mother was born in Grotta Minarda, not too far from my family's and my extended families' towns. We spoke the same dialect. Listening to him speak "our" Italian, I was carried back to my childhood. Even today when I am searching for a word that is NOT standard Italian, he will come up with it immediately. We have the same traditions; we can sing the same Italian/Neapolitan songs and amazingly enough we know all the great Italian baseball players on the Yankees and Red Sox.

One street away from where Father grew up on Charter Street is Sheafe Street where my Uncle Tony Polcari grew up. Uncle Tony was the best man I ever knew. He was born in 1908. Father Claude, the other best man I know, was born in 1934. Uncle Tony's son, my cousin Tony, was born in 1936 and attended Christopher Columbus High School with Father Claude. So many connections in the North End.

Michelangelo School

St. Anthony's School

Copps Hill Terrace

Chapter One

The Beginning

Father Claude entered this world on July 28, 1934. The second youngest of six children born to Palma and Antonio Scrima. Palma had immigrated from Grotta Minarda, province of Avellino and Antonio from Ariano de Puglia. Father Claude was then known as Stanley (changed from Stanzilavo on his birth certificate), his sisters were Connie, Silvia, Gilda, and Mary and his older brother was Mikey. Most of the children's names were anglicized. Stanley's parents were married at Sacred Heart Church and Stanley was Baptized there as well. He grew up in the North End of Boston on 48 Charter Street across from the Michelangelo School. The family's first floor flat in the tenement had six rooms and the tenement itself had 5 floors. These were the times of cold-water (no heat, no hot water) flats. The toilet was in the hallway that would often be shared by two families that lived on the same floor. There was no TV, no telephone and ventilation was poor. Family lived nearby. Everyone knew everybody and knew their business as well! If a child wasn't behaving, a neighbor would quickly tell the offending child's mother as soon as she could yell out the window. That solved the problem of no telephones. But as sparse as this all sounds today, it was a time where family meant everything, as did your traditions and neighborhood.

Father's family spoke Italian and English at home and kept all the Italian traditions of their towns in Italy! Christmas Eve for Stanley was the most joyous Holy Day of all. La Vigilia, the Feast of the Seven Fishes on Christmas Eve was celebrated and Baby Jesus would be born. Being Italian and treasuring Christmas Eve are two precious gifts given to us, Father would tell me. And, he would then add living in the North End was "the frosting on the cake"!

The Depression Era's scourge did not skip many tenements, if any. Few people in the North End were making ends meet. Stanley would shine shoes in Scollay Square. Each shoeshine cost 10 cents and any money that could help the family of eight was greatly needed. Stanley's father was fortunate to have a job with the railroad. Ten-hour workdays were the norm. "Overtime" was a blessing! If it was available and offered to you, you immediately took it. Overtime could mean more food on the table. "We needed the extra bucks" said Father Claude. Stanley's mother cooked, cleaned, and cared for her six children. Palma was an excellent cook and could miraculously stretch the food they had and turn it into a sumptuous meal.

The first three children went to public school and as Stanley's father got raises from the New Haven Railroad the next three children attended Saint Anthony's School. They were taught by Franciscan nuns who at that time were mostly Irish. The students were almost all Italian immigrants or children of immigrants and most came to school speaking English and Italian. The Scrima children did well in their studies. However, Stanley had a little problem with mathematics which will be discussed in a later chapter.

Playing outside was a glorious and carefree time. There was a playground at school and also up on Charter Street there was Slide Park. (Copp's Hill). Stanley and his friends made up games and played softball. Stanley's position was shortstop. In the winter all the kids played in the snow. Slide Park was aptly named! The children always answered the snow-laden park's summons to come and play. They would all slide, yelling at the top of their lungs as they slid down the hill on cardboard. No Flexible Flyers back in the 30s and 40s. And even if there were, no one had the money to purchase a sled!

Stanley had some great childhood friends, and they all went to school together as well. Sonny Piazza was the exception!

Sonny Piazza lived at 47 Charter Street right across from Stanley. They became best friends. Sonny would get into a bit of trouble at St. Anthony's School and also at the Michelangelo School. School wasn't his special calling. Therefore, Sonny began his work career at a young age. His father, a fisherman, was from Sicily, and his mother was born in Boston, but her family came from the province of Avellino, where so many of us came from.

I think Sonny rivals Father Claude for his ability to tell stories. He is worthy of his own book, as Father Claude's nephew Jim Pasto, said to me. I heartily agree after just having one long phone conversation with Sonny Piazza, I could envision the chapters. Most of his stories were hilarious.

One day Stanley wanted to visit the seminary in Andover and he asked Sonny to get him a bike. The bike magically appeared, and both he and Sonny (on his own bike) set out on the long ride to Andover. After visiting, the priests wouldn't allow them ride back to Boston in the dark on their bikes, as it was obviously too dangerous, Consequently, they had to stay the night at the seminary The next morning, they biked back to the North End, with dogs chasing after them to make a bad situation worse. Upon arrival at home, Stanley's mother was "really mad", Father Claude told me. She had no idea where he had been.

The best friends went to The North Bennett Street Summer Camp in Boxford. Many families took advantage of that program; my mother loved it, my aunt did not, but that is another story. Stanley and Sonny also spent three summers in Littleton, NH at Caddy Camp in the 40s. Their mentor was John P. Dexter, the Director. The boys were paid 50 cents to caddy 18 holes of golf. No tips. I asked Sonny what was the best thing he liked about the Camp. He readily answered, "The food". I was amazed at his answer. He said, "At the Caddy Camp there was food, and back home we all were rationed, food was scarce. I felt ashamed that I hadn't remembered that. I thought about it for a moment .... lack of food. Depression, World War 2, not the best of times at all.

Sonny got a bit somber as he continued to talk. He asked me, "Do you know what I did when Stanley went to Canada?" I said no. His answer was. "I cried, I was losing my best friend".

During these days in the North End, there wasn't time to be lonely or bored. The days were always filled with chores, homework, shining shoes, helping Mama and playing games with the boys. No one thought they were missing out on anything because basically everyone was in the same economic place. That place was called "The North End".

Sacred Heart Church

Stanley (to be Father Claude) with Niece Joan

Antonio, Jim Pasto, Stanley

Gilda, Connie, Palma, Antonio, Mikey, Mary, Stanley and Silvia

Chapter Two

School and Beyond
Becoming a Priest

Stanley had some great friends near his flat and also in school. He enjoyed school, but thought the Nuns were too strict. "But they did care about us", he added upon reflection. At that time, the majority of the Franciscan nuns were Irish. (*When my mother arrived from Italy she attended St. Anthony's School as well. However, the nuns were Italian, and many subjects were taught in Italian.) During Stanley's time at St. Anthony's, he remembers Sister Mary Yolanda who was Italian and taught Italian. Stanley loved the class and did very well. He has fond memories of her, even though she was strict. All the children respected her and learned "the good" Italian. My cousin Ron Polcari also loved Sister Mary Yolanda. So, she had quite a following.

As he grew older, Stanley began to have the feeling in his heart that he would like to become a priest. He had strong devotions to the Saints as many Italians had. His favorite Saints were:

Saint Anthony: Number one!
Saint Claude: His patron, as he was named after him when he became a priest.
Saint Thérèse of Lisieux: The Little Flower.
and *Saint Francis* of course.

By eighth grade, he thought that he wasn't smart enough to become a priest and he learned that the Brothers of Charity had a junior novitiate that began after eighth grade. There was a problem in that the novitiate was near Montreal Canada and the language spoken was French! Although Stanley didn't have the confidence to strive to become a priest, he was not daunted by the fact of going to a new country and having to learn French very quickly. So, it was off to the North he ventured.

After year one he changed his mind! His confidence grew and he prayed to God that he would have the ability to complete the rigorous studies needed to become a priest. He returned home to the North End and attended Christopher Columbus High School, which was also staffed by Franciscans as was his church Saint Leonard's. He had many chats with Father Anzalone OFM, who counseled Father to follow the path of the priesthood and believe that he was capable of the work he would be required to complete in the seminary. Slowly he started to believe that yes! he could become a priest and God would help him! After graduating from high school, he entered the novitiate of the Franciscans in Troy, New York. He then continued on to the Seminary of the Franciscans of the Immaculate Conception Province in Wappingers Falls, New York. His favorite subject was theology. He was ordained a Franciscan priest on May 21, 1961.

When I asked Father Claude why he chose to become a Franciscan he quickly answered, "I was drawn to and strongly believe in the Franciscan Way of Life". So, I researched a little and found what Father was talking about. And if you know Father Claude you can understand why this life would appeal to him. To me he is the epitome of all things good and that is the Franciscan Way of Life.

Franciscans believe in living a simple life. They avoid materialism and consumerism, and they focus on the things that are truly important, such as relationships and spiritual growth. Franciscans are committed to promoting peace and justice in the world. They work to address the root causes of poverty, inequality, and violence. Franciscans believe that we have a responsibility to care for the Earth. They work to protect the environment and promote sustainable living.

Franciscan
Center, Tampa, Florida

One day in December I was visiting Father, and we were walking from the Memory Care Unit to a Singalong (we love singalongs) in another part of the complex. We usually walk arm in arm. I don't know why I would think that I could even remotely steady him! But nevertheless, I think it was a comfort to both of us. On the other side of the corridor there was an older man on a stretcher who was obviously not doing well. He was very thin and had a faraway look in his eyes and his pupils were very cloudy. Father Claude walked right over to the man and cupped his large hands around the gentleman's head, with each long finger outstretched. There wasn't a part of the man's head that was untouched. This was done without a moment's hesitation, and I almost took a tumble as Father was walking at a good clip. I am Italian and it is in our genes, or at least in my family's genes to get emotional. Tears started falling down my cheeks. This act of kindness was intrinsic, without forethought. I think that was when I realized that Father Claude was really a special person.

I later asked about this event, and he remembered it vividly! "Of course I do, I gave him a blessing". So much for loss of short-term memory.

When I visit Father Claude, I make him lunch, always Italian food. His favorite is eggplant parmigiana. His highest compliment to me was that the eggplant tasted just like his mother's. But some days I brought pizza. He loved his pizza too and he would say "questa pizza è molto buona". He would ask for a half a slice more but end up eating the other half as well!

During our lunches I would ask questions that I needed for this book. If you really know Father Claude, he loves to tell stories! One question that was always on my mind was, "What do you like best about being a priest?" He answered without hesitation, "Helping people, ministering to their needs and giving the Sacraments".

Many of his parishioners' remembrances of Father Claude will be mentioned in another chapter, but one remembrance hit me to the core of who Father Claude is.

"He told us when you give a donation to someone in the streets, give it out of love and don't question what they will do with the money." **Rose Gianmarco.**

He fervently believed we should love all people. Not judging, not assuming, not condemning, just giving love. The Franciscan way of life.

Directly after Father Claude was ordained, he was assigned to teach at an all-boys Catholic high school, Serra Catholic High School in Pennsylvania. He taught, French, Religion and Latin primarily. He loved teaching and as a teacher myself, I can tell he was an excellent teacher. He loved his students!

Father told me he would often give advice to his students and extra help to those who were falling behind in their studies. When faced with boys who were misbehaving in class, he would give out detention but that was not very often.

Zia Carmella, Antonio, Father Claude, Palma, and Connie

Antonio, Father Claude, Palma, and Joan

Father Claude and Nieces

I asked about how he prepared his homilies: He didn't take long to answer. "I applied the gospel to the present day and gave examples from my experiences from everyday life and always kept in mind what my parishioners were going through". Father did mention that when he celebrated the Mass in Italian, he had to write out the homilies in Italian. But the homilies in English were "off the cuff" as he phrased it. I had to laugh. No one can beat Father Claude "off the cuff!" I brought up "Am I talking to someone?", which he changed to "somebody". Apparently, he would add this to his homilies when he thought it was necessary to wake up the parishioners who were not paying attention or perhaps a little sleepy from the night before! This phrase would definitely get their attention!

I asked, "What would you like to say to your parishioners now?" Father replied:

"Thank you to everyone! I miss you! I wish all of you happiness, health and a long life. I know you will continue to love God and your neighbor. Please pray for Peace in our world today."

At Serra Franciscan High School in Pennsylvania

Chapter Three

Father Claude's Contributions to the North End and the Franciscans

Father Claude was also assigned to teach at Christopher Columbus High School, the Franciscan high school for boys in the North End, which he had graduated from in the 1950's. He loved teaching French! He was still fluent from his days at the Junior Novitiate in Sorel, Montreal. He also taught Latin and Religion. He had a special gift for learning languages. But don't ask him about anything mathematical! Father insisted on telling me on numerous occasions that he was deficient in mathematical skills.

If there was ever a problem with one of the students, it was almost a certainty Father Claude would know the family or a relative of the family. So, a dynamic evolved: how a troublesome student behaved was based on the knowledge that Father Claude would make sure that the student's family knew what was going on. Basically, to the North End students, it was as if your family was teaching you. You didn't get away with anything. And it was not a one-way street. Father Claude also reported back to the families the successes the students had as well.

He loved being with people. A familiar sight was to see Father Claude walking the streets of the North

End. Everyone knew and loved him, and they would stop to talk, hug and wish him well. It was a Father Claude Traffic Jam! He knew most families and would ask about how little "Joey" or "Gina" was doing. A frequent visitor to his parishioners' homes, he would check to see how the infirm and elderly were doing, sit and have a cup of coffee with them and chat. And oh, how he could chat!

What a gift and blessing he was to Christopher Columbus High School, Saint Leonard's Church and the whole North End.

He was assigned to the Andover Seminary for a number of years and taught Latin, Italian and French to the seminarians. His family would often go to visit him there and would enjoy the country atmosphere of the seminary grounds and surrounding buildings. The facility was St. Francis Seraphic Seminary (River Road, Andover) - Operated by the Order of Friars Minor of the Province of the Immaculate Conception from 1930-1977. When the seminary closed in 1977, it was then operated as the Franciscan Retreat and Conference Center. Father would conduct numerous Retreats there for his Parishioners. He was an admired and acclaimed retreat master and preacher of missions in parishes within the Archdiocese of Boston and elsewhere.

Father Claude was selected by the Franciscan Provence of the Immaculate Conception to be the head of the Third Order of Saint Francis. The Secular Franciscans, also known as the Third Order Secular, are allowed to marry. It is a group comprising of religious laymen and women who focus on mirroring the spirit of St. Francis by carrying out works of social service, charity, and teaching, just like Saint Francis did when he lived. He held this position for two years. This order is seeing a resurgence even at Saint Leonard's Church. My grandmother became a Third Order member and was also buried in the brown robes of the Franciscans. Last week, I showed Father Claude my grandmother's member card that I always have with me. We both got a bit nostalgic.

The Bronze Sculpture

Dear Father Claude,

    A few years ago, your nephew, Jimmy Pasto, introduced us. I had heard from so many people what a delightful man you are and are loved by so many in the North End. Because Jimmy and I were good friends, he and I would visit you at the Friary or have lunch with you at Bella Vista. I had the pleasure of listening to you recount many wonderful stories of growing up in the North End. One story has especially stayed with me; how the kids had different corners in the North End based upon where they lived, however for the most part they still got along.
    One day Jimmy and I made plans to join you in North Square for a special surprise. In 2019, Ann and

Jeremy from A & J Artist had designed and installed four special historical bronze sculptures in the famous North Square. We met them there during the inauguration and dedication by Mayor Walsh. After the ceremony we asked you to scan the sculpture of the spy glasses and to look closely at one of the portraits etched on the sculpture. Well, were you beyond surprised to see yourself etched into the bronze instrument! This was one more way you are honored for your lifetime work at Saint Leonard's. Of course, as is your "style" you felt very humbled by the gesture.

It gave Jimmy and me great pleasure to know that you will always be a permanent part of the North End and your presence is firmly established in your beloved North End.

Fondly,
Tom Damigella

Jim Pasto, Father Claude, Tommy Damigella, Ann and Jeremy (A & J Artist, sculptors)

Bronze Sculpture

Christopher Columbus High School Reunion
photo courtesy of Arthur Sonny Lauretano

Chapter Four

THE TERRIBLE FALL
Stories by Andy Gaus

One afternoon, Father Claude was visiting me, and I invited him to stay for dinner. He was glad to accept the invitation. You must understand that Father Claude's notion of a nice dinner invitation is where he brings the food and cooks it. He set out on a walk to the grocery store to get some food to cook a fine dinner for us both. He didn't come back all evening long and all night long. I had no idea whether he was alive or dead. It was next morning before I was able to reach someone at St. Leonard's and find out that he had taken a terrible fall. Father Claude told me afterwards that he started feeling a little woozy as he was walking but decided to continue. Then he blacked out and fell face forward onto the concrete. After several stints in the hospital and rehab facilities, Father Claude is healthy again. However, that fall put an end to 60 years of active pastoral service, including the sermons that many parishioners drove in from the suburbs to hear. He no longer walks from the North End to Charlestown and back to get a little exercise.

I got to know Father Claude some forty years ago while serving as an organist at Saint Leonard's. Besides playing the organ, I sang the services as best I could. I never did have a good singing voice, so Father Claude, who of course sings very well, if he wasn't celebrating the service himself, would come and stand by the organ and relieve me of the singing duties. I was very happy to relinquish it to him. It gave me a strong sense of what kind of person he was. He didn't want to simply take a rest between services if there was something he could do to lighten my labors and improve everyone else's churchgoing experience. I knew then that I didn't want to lose touch with such a remarkable person. I am honored that he felt the same way. After my service as organist was finished, we would still meet now and then for coffee or a meal. Every year Father Claude would remind me when the annual spaghetti dinner for St. Anthony's Feast was coming up, so we always saw each other there even if we hadn't seen each other for a while. We have been friends for forty years, and in all those years he has continued to be the same person I first came to know and respect. I have rarely had an occasion to ask him for help, because he generally offers his help before I have time to ask for it.

EARLY YEARS

Father Claude has shared with me many memories of growing up. He was born in Readville on July 28, 1934, to Antonio and Palma Uva Scrima, immigrants from the Avellino & Puglia regions of Italy who met in the United States. His father worked for a while as a gravedigger before settling into a career on the railroad. He was hoping his son would follow him into a railroad career and was disappointed when it turned out that his son was needed elsewhere.

Young Stanley—that was his name back then—along with four older sisters, Connie, Sylvia, Mary, and Jill, and an older brother, Mike, lived with their parents in an apartment on Charter Street in Boston's North End. It was cold. The closest thing to storm windows was stuffing rags into the chinks where the wind was blowing through. There were a couple of stoves but no central heating, so some rooms were miserably cold. Beds were sometimes warmed by heating a brick, wrapping it in a towel, and placing it at the foot of the bed.

One good way to get warm was to go to Aunt Carmela's house and play in her basement. She was a little more well-to-do and had a furnace. The other solution was to hang out in the kitchen. Stanley spent a lot of time in the kitchen watching his mother cook. He credits her as the reason that he became a fine cook himself.

Palma was a very good cook. On a limited budget she fed a family of eight—very well. The food was delicious, and they were never hungry. And certainly, the food was fresh—fresh bread from the bakery, fresh produce from the grocery, and fresh meat from the butcher. As for the chicken, by today's standards, it was too fresh for comfort. Father Claude was sometimes sent to the market to get chicken. He would point out the chicken he wanted. They would slit its throat, remove internal organs, and rub the outside against a rotating drum with metal nubs on its surface to strip off the feathers. That was one way. The other way was to bring the squawking bird home alive and take it to Aunt Carmela, the same aunt with the warm basement. She was also useful in turning live chickens into dead chickens, something Father Claude's mother couldn't bring herself to do. How fresh was the chicken Father Claude grew up with? So fresh it just died.

There was no shower in the Scrimas' house. To take a shower, you went to the bathhouse down the street. You couldn't shower daily: there were Men's Nights and Ladies' Nights. On the other hand, the ocean beach was just down the street, easy walking distance.

Customs were different back then. Father Claude related that at Italian weddings he attended as a youth, it was perfectly normal for men to dance with each other. What was not perfectly normal was for a man to ask another man's wife to dance. You didn't do that if you knew what was good for you.

He was a shoeshine boy in Scollay Square, now Government Center. If he could bring home a dollar, earned one dime at a time, it was a real contribution to the family's economy.

Father Claude started to answer the calling he felt in his high-school years. He originally traveled to Canada, intending to join the order of the Brothers of Charity there. However, after a year of study, he had a life-changing conversation with Father Edmund Anzalone, then stationed at Saint Leonard's. Father Edmund asked young Stanley why he was studying to be a brother and not a priest. He answered that he would like to be a priest but felt daunted when he looked at all the studying required. Father Edmund replied, "If God wants you to be a priest He will get you through your studies," and so it was.

Andy and Father Claude

JUNIORATE OF THE BROTHERS OF CHARITY
WEST NEWBURY, MASS.
APPLICATION FORM

1. Name *Stanley J. Scrima*
2. Address *48 Charter Street*
3. Age *15* Birthplace *Readville, Mass*
4. Your Father (*yes*) and your mother (*yes*) are alive?
5. How many brothers (*1*) and sisters (*4*) have you?
6. Name of school you attend *Columbus Catholic High*
7. In what grade are you? *Junior*
8. Do you know anybody in the Juniorate? *no*
9. Why do you wish to enter the Juniorate? *yes*
10. Who advised you to do so? *none*
11. How long ago since you first thought of becoming a Brother? *Just a year ago*
12. Do both your parents approve of this intention? *yes*
13. Are your parents in need of your help? *no*
14. Are there any priests (*no*) religious (*no*) in your family? (*Cousin*)
15. Have you already asked to be admitted elsewhere? *no*
16. Are you in good health? *✓* Ever been seriously sick? *no*
17. Are you able to obey? *✓* Ready to put up with others? *✓*
18. To whom may we apply for references concerning your conduct?
My School, or parish (St. Leonard's Boston)

PROMISE

If the Superiors of the Juniorate find that I possess the requisite aptitudes to become a Brother of Charity and if the way of living of the Juniorate suits me—with the help of God's grace and the consent of my parents—I bind myself, on my own word of honor, to follow courageously God's call to a higher life.
(This promise does not bind in conscience.)

Signature *Stanley J. Scrima*

IMMIGRATION BRANCH
TEMPORARY ENTRY RECORD

Port *Sutton, P.Q.* Date *Jan. 21/50*
Name *Scrima, Stanley J.*
Address *118 Charter St., Boston Mass*
Birthplace *Boston, Mass*
Age *15* Citizenship *U.S.A.*
Object in coming to Canada *Student*
Destined to *Mt. St. Bernard School*
Address *Sorel, P.Q.*
Temporary entry until *June 30/50*
Signature of passenger *Stanley J. Scrima*
Signature of officer *[illegible]*

Please have your departure from Canada verified by a Canadian Immigration Officer who will release you of further responsibility of disposing of this record. If that is not practicable please have departure verified by a Canadian Customs Officer, or the United States Immigration or Customs Service at the U.S. port of entry, or by the Conductor, Purser, or other person in charge if you travel by public conveyance. THEN MAIL THIS RECORD TO THE CANADIAN IMMIGRATION OFFICE AT THE PORT WHERE YOU ENTERED CANADA.

Chapter Five

North Enders and Friends Fond Memories and Tributes

Fr. Claude is beloved by us North Enders because he is a beautiful, loving, gentle hearted man who humbly serves God and would always tell it like it is. He was always direct in his homilies and used his humor and no-nonsense approach to pastorally help many people.

Also Fr. Antonio said (when I first started) that in the sixteen years of living with Fr Claude that he was always a joy to parish life. **Fr. Michael Della Penna: Pastor Saint Leonard's Church.**

My dealings with Father Claude were numerous. Many were at the North End Nursing Home where my mother was a resident.

I would see Fr. Claude numerous evenings because I was there every night for 8 years. But unfortunately, he was there on "Official Duties" giving last rites. I would say to him "Father I like seeing you but not in these circumstances. He would just smile and give me and my mom a blessing. I would also see Fr. Claude in the streets when I would take my mom for a walk when the weather was nice. On those instances I would say "Hi, good to see you here and not there". **John Pagliuca**

Dear Father Claude, growing up in the North End with your guidance was truly a blessing. Sharing your birth with my mother was always "special". The many discussions we had regarding world events and breaking bread together at my home with the family will always be cherished memories. With love and prayers, **Grazie Mille, Angela Capucci Aquilino and Family**

I love you and I miss you! **Phyllis**

Am I talking to Somebody? You always said that during Mass! **Doreen Merola**

Father Claude, we miss you here in the North End. We remember you always! **P. Bono**

Father Claude, you are greatly missed. We always enjoyed your homilies.

Father Claude, we are so grateful for your devotion to God and the community. We so enjoyed your legendary sermons and found such great example and guidance from your words of wisdom. **Tony and Loretta Cannistraci**

Father Claude you are an "unfiltered voice of God". You are the reason our family joined Saint Leonard's Parish. **The Tannoury Family**

Father Claude, Collette and I moved here from Connecticut and New York. The saddest moment we had was leaving our amazing priest, until we met you! **Collette Divitto and Rosemary A.**

Father Claude, I miss your daily blessing you bestowed on me when I saw you. **Lena Piciardo** *(Father Ronald Siciliano's cousin.)*

Father Claude, thank you for all your homilies. I'll never forget "The Tongue" How it can start World War III, and the stories you told of your father. Thanks for so much. Love you always, **Anthony Cogliani**

Dearest Father Claude, I'll always remember you as the kind soul I encountered in the parking lot as I first started my job at St. Leonard's Parish. P.S. We all appreciate your beautiful smile. **Theresa Ngyen**

Father Claude, you always have a warm smile. You remembered everything I ever said to you! You always listened! Thank you, **Bonnano Family**

We will always remember you! **La scuola d' Italiano**

You bring joy to my life. **Peggy Fucillo**

God Bless You'! *Christine Teta Capillo*

Dear Father Claude, I have so many fond memories of you! Where do I begin? I had the honor of having you Baptize my son almost 40 years ago. You were always so pleasant to get to know! I still remember volunteering at the Bookstore and you would stop by on your daily walks to chat with me in Italian. Can you imagine that an American - born can speak Italian! I enjoyed attending 10:30a.m. Italian Mass when you celebrated and hearing your homily in fluent Italian. You were so interesting to listen to.

Thank you for all you did and continue to do for our Faith community. Know that I am praying for you. Lovingly, *Assunta Guarino D'Alelio*

Grazie per la benedizione sulla generazione di mi familia. E anche la gloria di tua sorella Silvia. Siamo Pugliese. Mille Grazie! *Anna*

Padre Claude, da anni e anni sei il miglior prete della chiesa di San Leonardo. Ti piacciono le mie melanzane marinate e hai amato così tanto mio figlio Paulo. Ti vogliamo bene! Ti prendevi cura di tutti! Siamo tutti pregando per te. *Natalina D'amore Tizzzano*

Caro padre Claude, Mi manchi tanto. Ti conosco da molto tempo. Sei un Padre meraviglioso, forte e intelligente. Conosci mia madre Michelina e mio padre

Angelo. Anche tu sei stato a casa mia molte volte! Ti amo! **Emilia Cataldo Martignetti** Endicott Street. / Montefalcione.

Father Claude, I have been in Food Service my life! Literally 45 Years! One of your homilies just resonated with me.: "Jesus was a server. We need to serve!" This was a nice connection because a lot of people are in Food Service. And I think you really struck something with a lot of us. **Mark Platt**

God Bless, Fr. Claude! **Jeanette Puopolo DiBisceglia**

God bless Father Claude, a great priest! **Dottie Simbo**

Fr. Claude, You used to give the best homilies and made us want to go to church and leave Mass with a good feeling.

You kept us on our toes when every once in a while, you would say "Manca per la capa"(unbelievable). We laughed. It sounded so funny coming from you. "Am I talking to someone?" when you would recount how families were not talking to each other for some insignificant thing that happened 20 years ago! You always stressed families to put their bad feelings aside and be civil to one another and bring harmony within their families.

You told us when you give a donation to someone in the streets, give it out of love and don't question what they will do with the money. You always greeted us with kindness when we met you on the street.

Asking how me and my family were. Viva Fr. Claude!
Rose Gianmarco

Dear Father Claude, we love you and miss you and your wonderful homilies. Am I Talking to Someone? Love, **Doreen Gianmarco**

Padre Claudio, Ti recordo con tanto affeto e spero ele stai bene. Sei sempre nel nostro cuori. Sei el miglore! **Lina (Osteria)**

Great priest, Father. **Dolores Maniscalco D'alfonso**

Dear Father Claude, one of the most frequent sermons you would give was concerning the "accumulation of wealth". Your retort was something like this:" When was the last time you saw a U-Haul following a hearse?" I love you; you are a special priest with all your wisdom. May God bless you, Father Claude, forever! Peace and Love, **Mary T. Savino**

Father Claude, I personally recall your generosity in sitting down with my son, Ezio, before first communion. Ezio did not attend school in the North End, and because of the commute from Cambridge, arrived home at the end of the day too late to attend the required CCD classes at St. John's School. I had permission to "homeschool" him in Catholic doctrine, supplemented by Sunday School at St. Joseph's in the West End. To make matters worse, Ezio decided at age seven that he didn't believe in any of it and kept us guessing as to whether or not he would consent to the ceremony. At my wit's end, I asked your nephew, Prof. James Pasto, to see if you would be willing to meet with Ezio and sort things out. Jim kindly facilitated contact with you, and even though it was in the midst of Easter season Fr. Claude, you found time on 29 April 2014 to meet with Ezio at the rectory and hear his concerns. You reported to me later that you had really enjoyed speaking with Ezio and found him remarkably thoughtful and aware for his age. Ezio was deemed doctrinally sound for First Communion, and we still have the felt banner he made with the dove and chalice and his name "Salimbeni". This isn't all: Ezio did, in the end, grow into the Catholic faith and became the head reader at chapel in his boarding school. I am grateful that you, Fr. Claude did not give up on him when we were all about to. It gave Ezio the opportunity to find his own way in Christ. **Jessica Della Russo**

Dear Father Claude, people say that one person can't make a difference in the world, but my husband and I know that it isn't true, we've seen the difference that you made in our lives. You soothed Jimmy and myself with kind words and prayer throughout his illness and death. We appreciated you, Father Claude, for visiting us numerous times at home and at the hospital. Your genuine concern went a long way in helping cope with my grief. You helped me to remember that even though Jimmy is gone, his angel is always watching over.

You are truly a blessing to our church and made difficult days less stressful. We need more people like you, Father Claude in the world. I appreciated your kindness and thoughtfulness. **Barbara Coppola**

Dear Father Claude, I have such wonderful memories of you! **Pat Seanlow**

Dear Father Claude, I enjoyed every Mass and every story you told us! Miss you, **Romilda Locchi**

Dear Father Claude. you are a model priest and a great man! **Arthur Sonny Lauretano**, Christopher Columbus High School Graduate, F.O.N.E.

Dear Father Claude, you were my classmate at St Anthony's School. (I was asking about you!) God bless. **Rosemarie (Nastasi) Skiffington**

One cool priest!!!! I got to know Father Claude by being a customer in my store. Pleasant I might add. The more I saw him around the neighborhood, the more I got to know him. Then one day I'm standing outside my store talking with my mother and father and Father Claude walks by and he said hello to my mother. "Hi Josie!" Not as a priest, but as a regular neighborhood guy that grew up together as children. Come to find out, my mother and I know his sisters, but I didn't know they were related. I've known his nephew, Jimmy, since we were children. Father Claude's sister used to work at the nursing home where my parents ended up. I didn't go to church much, but when I went, it was usually a funeral mass. Father Claude always made the services comforting and interesting. Many times, he actually knew the deceased. I will always remember Father Claude as a cool neighborhood guy and priest. **Mark Petrigno**

God bless you Father Claude for answering His call to the priesthood. Happy 63rd Anniversary. Thank you for the many retreats at the Franciscan Center in Andover. May Our Lady always keep you protected beneath Her Holy Mantle. **Rosie Maminstine**

God Bless you Fr. Claude. **Joe Gaeta**

You are special! **Rosemary Mello**

Love you Fr. Claude GOD BLESS YOU! **Holly Marcus**

I have been blessed to share so many memories with you, Father Claude! Thank you's could never express my gratitude. **Reine Ella**

Congratulations, blessings and gratitude Father. **Kath Ca**

Dear Fr. Claude,

Congratulations on your 90th birthday from the Cortese/D'Alessandro Family! Our family has been so lucky to be parishioners at St. Leonard's Church during your years as a priest and pastor! We remember your wonderfully sensitive and uplifting sermons and how you cared for and engaged with the entire community and our family. Your energy and enthusiasm always made everyone you interacted with feel special. The genuine way you focused on helping anyone in need was indeed in the spirit of St. Francis. We loved your sense of humor and your beautiful stories. We appreciate your long friendship with our late great uncle, Bishop Bernardine Mazzarella, OFM, and our uncle, Fr. Francis X. D'Alessandro, OFM. We enjoyed your frequent visits with our parents, Nick and Cecilia Cortese, and our aunt Helen D'Alessandro at D'Alessandro's Religious Good Store (aka "the Saint Store") and our house on North Bennet St. It was always a treat to know you were coming to visit. Thank you for what you have done for the North End Community and the Franciscan Order of Priests! You have enriched our lives! We wish our parents and relatives were still around to celebrate with you. We know they are looking down on you with great reverence and joy! Sincerely, **Anthony Cortese, Palma Cortese, Luci Cortese, Nick Cortese, Jr., Frances Bechtold**

Chapter Six

Father Claude: Families' Stories

Father Claude's nieces and nephew had some great stories to tell. I am still laughing at some! He loved telling ghost stories. He made the stories up as he went along and created his own sound effects! What a joy it was for them to have Father Claude as an uncle. They loved him dearly and certainly have very fond memories of their younger years.

Contributed by Niece Lisa

Here are a couple of stories that Uncle used to tell over and over again about when he was a young boy. We never tired of hearing them.

You Breaka the Shirt

When my uncle was in Catholic grade school, he was taught by nuns from Ireland. He said they were very "tough". One day, one of the nuns was so disappointed in Uncle's incorrect answers that she roughed him up a bit and tore his shirt.

Uncle went home to his mother and told her that he was not going back to that school no matter what she said (my grandmother, his mother was an Italian immigrant and spoke little to no English). My grandmother was distraught! No matter what she said,

Uncle was not budging, so she called her sister Carmella (to Uncle, Zia Carmella) to go up to the school with Uncle and try to figure out what happened and smooth things over.

Uncle and Zia went to this particular nun and had a conversation in the hallway that went something like this:

Nun: Stanley, now who is this lovely woman you have brought here today?
Uncle: This is my Aunt Zia Carmella.
Nun: Well, hello, Mrs. Zingamella. What can I do for you today?
Zia: The mother, she cry because you breaka the shirt.
Nun: Stanley. What stories have you been telling? Did I break your shirt? Did you make your dear mother cry?
Uncle: frightened to death, responded "I don't know" in a very sheepish way.
Nun: Oh Mrs. Zingamella. Please tell Stanley's dear mother that nothing of the kind happened and that we will take excellent care of him here.
Zia: Okay. Thanka you.

When Uncle and the nun returned to the classroom, the nun said, "Well, class, it looks like we have a milquetoast here." and she gave him one good whack and sent him to his seat.

The Chalkboard

It was math time at school and Uncle was called to the blackboard to work out a problem he had no idea how to solve. He went up and wrote, erased, wrote, erased, and he could see out of the corner of his eye that the nun was getting more and more steaming mad. Finally, she took the chalk from him and said, "Why you dirty, dirty thing," and started banging his head up against the chalkboard to the point where Uncle could actually see the chalk dust falling from the board.

Just at that time, the nun from the next room over came running in. "Sister Mary Margaret, I heard banging. Is everything alright?" The nun responded, "Why yes sister. I'm just banging Stanley's head against the wall." When I read this story to Father Claude, he added: And Sister Mary Margaret said: 'Well give him one for me'.

Poor Times

What is interesting to note is that there were six siblings. The first three went to public school, but as my grandfather received promotions on the railroad where he worked, he eventually became a foreman, and could afford to send the last three to Catholic school.

But times were very tough, and Uncle told us about how he would have to put cardboard in his shoes to cover the holes in the soles, and how they used to have to sleep with hot bricks in their beds because it was so cold (no heat).

Contributed by Niece Donna

Uncle Stanley

My Uncle, there are so many things to say about him and who he is, this book is going to be longer than the dictionary, so speaking. HA

Being a priest has its ups and downs in his family. From marrying all of his siblings, nieces, nephews, cousins (you get the picture) to burying all who passed as well. When he married me and my late husband Brian, everyone was more captivated by his sermon than the wedding Mass and forgot why they were there in the first place, even me, the BRIDE. I eventually had to cut him off because we only had the church for another 10 minutes to finish our vows.

Our family always looked forward to the many fun cookouts at the Andover Seminary (which I was convinced was haunted) with all of us playing lawn games and the other Franciscans joining our crazy group for a fun-filled Sunday. It was a time when we all got together to visit with Uncle and it wasn't for a wedding or wake. Some of my aunts and I would go to the seminary and take over the kitchen for "Spaghetti Dinners" that the Franciscans would hold. Uncle boasted that his family jumped in to help out with feeding all the people that came. I got stuck with the pots and pans.

Uncle had a knack of telling us the craziest ghost stories that he made up as he went along, convincingly with sound effects and all. We used to beg him to tell us a story every time. He loved to have us enthralled in his ghoulish ghost stories. I remember the "hook hand"! and he acted like he was the Wolfman in some, with scary faces and a sinister laugh. I always saw the man with the "hook hand" in my nightmares, thanks Uncle. At that age, I believed his stories. He made them sound so real and had such an effect on me that I couldn't use the ladies' room in the Seminary without 5 people with me. How can such a gentle man have the scariest ghost stories?

During a memorial for his sister, my mom Mary (Scrima) Greco, we had at St Leonard's Church (once again, buried another) he was just so humble and always kept it together for his family. Afterwards, a group of us walked about two blocks for pizza, maybe a 10-minute walk, TOOK 30+ MINUTES. Everyone in his path stopped him and chatted with him like he was the Governor. It was the same thing coming back. Let's just say the walk to and from lunch was longer than lunch. Even where he is at this time, we can't get down the hallway without stopping multiple times to chat with other residents. He would speak in Italian and French to some of the residents. He taught French to his students at the Seminary and always spoke fluent Italian, I took 3 years of French in high school for him and still to this day, still can't speak a sentence of it. He used to talk to me in French and I.....Sorry Uncle!!

Uncle Stanley loves his family more than life. People are drawn to him naturally because of his notoriety as well as his infectious personality, humble demeanor and compassion and has a sense of humor to boot. I'm happy to have the privilege of sharing some of the memorable things about a great man. I hope someday, you have that privilege too. God Bless

Contributed by Nephew Jim Pasto

Uncle Claude Stories

I first knew Father Claude as "Uncle Stanley." I remember knowing that he was a priest but as young children my cousins and I called him "Uncle Stanley." He was a great uncle.

He told the best ghost stories. He would tell them at my Aunt Connie's (his sister Concetta) in Saugus. It was usually me and my cousins, Jim and Deborah (two of Connie's kids). We would be in bed and Claude would sit on a chair in the darkened room and tell the story. It usually involved a young boy, 'Joey' might have been his name, and a cemetery and a walk home at night. The one I remember most is when Joey had to get home before a rainstorm and to do it, he had to take a short cut through the town cemetery. He was afraid but steeled himself to do it. As he walked across, he heard someone walking behind him – a man dragging his lame leg. Claude would do special effects with his leg, stomping it on the floor and dragging it, while also telling us what was going on in Joey's mind. He would also make a musical sound for effects, a sound that was very scary and which he gave at just the right time. Joey always made it safely home, but it was also always a close call.

This is the only ghost story I remember but I also remember him telling us one about a giant Godzilla-like creature that attacked the Mystic Bridge. Claude said that my father was driving on the bridge when the creature tried to grab him, but he avoided it by driving in a zig zag. I remember Father Claude moving his hand is a zig zag and saying "zoom, zoom, zoom." I remember running into the kitchen (we were at Connie's) and asking my father if this was true and him nodding that it was, aware that this was coming from one of Fr. Claude's stories.

I also remember a time when Fr. Claude, my cousin Steve and I went swimming at some flats in Revere (across from the old drive in). I remember how Steve and I were both impressed by how good a swimmer

Uncle and Jim Pasto

Uncle, Mario Pasto and Barbara Maldero

Joan, Connie, and Deb Zarella

Uncle and Niece Lisa Gurney

Niece Kathy and Nephew Mike

Claude was. There was a man in the water who shouted for help because he had a cramp. He was not drowning but in need of help and Claude swam out to do so. We were proud of him.

For a long time, he lived at the Seminary in Andover where he was a teacher. We would go there to see him and have family cookouts and after, play bocce or other games.

About 10 years ago, when he was with Fr. Antonio at St. Leonard's we used to meet regularly – at least twice a month for dinner. Occasionally, it would be late and as I live on the Cape, Father Claude would let me stay in one of the rooms on the third floor of the rectory (with Antonio's kind permission). It was nice at these times to speak with him as an adult. He really respected me and that meant a lot to me.

Mark Brunini, Jim Pasto, Amaya, Alisa, Lisa Gurney, Mario, Farther Claude, Mary, Julie Zarella, Joan Zarella, Deb Zarella, Dan Gurney and Joseph Di Gangi

Niece Deb and Uncle

Uncle and Cheryl

Jim, Uncle, Cheryl

Uncle and Lisa

89th Birthday Party

Uncle and Cousin Michael

Cousin Mark, Uncle and Nephew Daniel

Uncle and Niece Joan

December 2023

January 2024

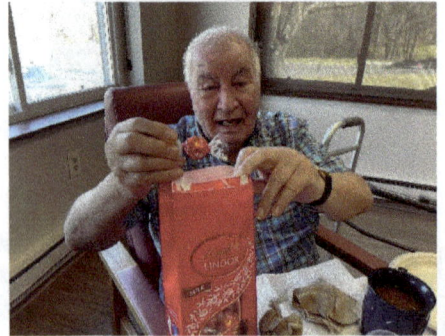

February 2024

July 2023

Chapter Seven

My Connection to Father Claude

As I mentioned, my first personal encounter with Father Claude was when he led me to where the statue of the Pieta had been sequestered. At that time, he didn't know me at all, and the thought that I just might, just maybe, take a certain statue out of hiding and return it to its former glory for all to see, didn't cross his mind. Ha!

After he was no longer serving as an active priest, I would make some food for him and bring chocolates to the friary. We would talk to each other in the parking lot and on the street of course. I'd ask if he got the chocolates and he would answer, "You're the one sending me all the food and chocolates. Thank you!" and then a hug and a blessing and another hug and another blessing! This would occur in the middle of Hanover Street!

I first started collecting signatures for Father Claude's birthday cards last summer (2023). This would be his first birthday away from his beloved Franciscan family. Then I started visiting him on a regular basis, every two weeks. His is such a friendly and caring man. I kept thinking that many more people should know him and about him. I wanted to tell his story as best I could, and a book slowly began to take shape.

The holidays are hard for me, but when I was visiting Father Claude, we had some Holiday fun. We decorated his tree that the Activity Coordinators had bought for his room. My neighbors gave me ivory and gold star quilted ornaments embroidered with PEACE and JOY. I also brought a small wooden Nativity. We sang, danced and even went to activities that the Manor had for its residents. I was having a good time "Walking In A Winter Wonderland" and I think Father Claude enjoyed having me to accompany him.

Some Reflections on Visits

Father Claude Friday March 7, 2024

Father Claude loves Chinese Food. As a surprise, his good friend Andy and I took him out to a highly praised restaurant, artfully adorned with Chinese Statues and paintings. We were seated in a comfortable red leather booth and given chopsticks. and hot oolong tea and little teacups. Father was eager to order his favorite appetizers and main entree. When the food arrived, Father used his chopsticks adroitly! He ate all his food and some of mine! Then, I was shocked! Father knows a few words of Mandarin Chinese and spoke pleasantries in Chinese to all the Chinese waitstaff that was passing by our booth! He speaks English, Italian, French, Latin and okay Spanish. Now I can add Mandarin to the list.

When visiting Father Claude, we always sing. He loves songs from the old days, Christmas carols and songs, hymns (How did I remember them?) But I did, even the ones in French, which delighted Father Claude to no end. Currently he has developed a fondness for the new song by Il Volo, "Capolavoro".

Warning! I play music when I am driving and it is loud, obscenely loud, as my cousin reminds me every time she hears my car approaching her house. "Capolavoro" was blasting as Father Claude got into the car on our way back from lunch. I asked him if he could understand the words. He answered "più o meno", more or less. "Do you recognize the word *Capolavoro*?" He is thoughtfully listening to Il Volo singing the following lyrics:

"E all'improvviso tu, tu Cadi dal cielo come un capolavoro"
(*And suddenly, you, you Fall from the sky like a masterpiece!*)

Father Claude turns to me without literally missing a beat and says "Masterpiece" I then say to him, "tu, tu!" He replies "no! tu tu! "…..singing right along with Il Volo.

Father Claude is a Masterpiece, You. You!

La musica è la magia che solleva l'anima e la fa gridare di gioia!

(Music is the magic that lifts the soul and makes it shout with joy!)

Father Claude Friday March 28, 2024

I have always thought that the relationship of Italians and their food was overplayed. But family and food has got me thinking, maybe it is more than just the way Italians are pigeonholed into just food loving people, with nothing else to offer. There just may be something more meaningful in that Prince Spaghetti commercial "Anthony". I loved that commercial as did the whole North End.

Before Easter, I had planned to bring Father Claude my homemade Pizza Cheina, but I opted for a variation. Yes, thinking about food and what to bring Father is always a priority when I visit. So, I went with some of the ingredients in Pizza Cheina. He loved it. The food, jump started Father to talk about his Easters and our family traditions. Since our families' towns in Italy are close to one another, we really are used to the same foods, prepared the same way and the food actually bonds us, brings us closer. I know that sounds a little strange, but when I saw Father Claude light up when he saw the array of olives I brought, they put him over the moon!

This really made me realize that food is an excellent catalyst that opens the door for all sorts of conversations and elicits emotions and memories that have long been forgotten. Needless to say, we had long conversations about past Easters, family get-togethers and the importance of Easter to our heritage and faith.

Father Claude Friday April 17, 2024

Pizza Day! I was delayed a bit visiting Father, but he was sitting right in the hallway, resting in a comfortable lounge chair, awaiting my entrance. He was sitting by himself, as all the residents were in the dining room. His eyes grew larger when he saw the familiar pizza box! Perhaps there was a bit of impatience as well? I was late and he was hungry! Trying to balance the pizza and my laptop at the same time, I was able to carry it all to the awaiting table, fortunately avoiding a catastrophe of epic proportions.

Father, as was always his refrain when eating pizza, kept on saying "la pizza è buona" and "no, I can't have anymore". Then I'd hear "maybe one more" and a bit later, "Can I have one more piece"! He then ate the mandarin orange and had a humongous chocolate chip cookie from Whole Foods. Always a smile on his face, he would welcome each resident when they came into the sunroom while we were eating lunch. We sang Capolavoro and read the lyrics

I had printed out. We watched and sang Mario Lanza Video of Sorrento to end our lunch. Singing is a joy to him, and it helps with speech and language. He thinks he can't dance, but we do, especially to "O sole mio".

We moved from the sunroom as Father said he was getting a little tired and may take a nap. I cleaned up, but instead of going back to his room he sat in the hallway, a gathering spot for the residents. Then I heard Father Claude asking the couple sitting next to him if they would like a slice of pizza. The wife needed to cut the slice in half to feed her husband, who was unable to feed himself. I cut it for her, and she helped feed her husband. Apparently, Father wanted to make sure everyone ate that afternoon, and he too ate another slice of pizza!

Father Claude Friday April 26, 2024

Traffic was kind to me as I traveled west on the Mass Pike. I parked in my usual spot and grabbed all my bags and quickly headed in to see Father Claude. He anxiously greeted me with "What do you have today Peggy"? Apparently, the mention of Eggplant Parmigiana was music to his ears, as he quickly tried to get up from the comfortable chair without the use of his walker, to help me with my parcels. He was delighted with the Menu for today and gave me the highest compliment any Italian cook can get. "Peggy, as always, this is so good, it is just the way my mother made it"! I knew It couldn't have been bad because he devoured three sandwiches and ate a numerous variety of olives.

We had to get some work done on the upcoming book and as we began, Father's friend Andy came in to join us! That was a blessing, as we got to laugh a lot learning about Father's love or lack thereof for Mathematics. I can relate to Father's disdain of anything mathematical, but he does take it to new levels. As you read in another chapter, I believe this all goes back to an incident in Elementary School. But please note as a counterbalance, Father can speak four languages.

We talked about the cover of the book and what pictures he would like. We bantered back and forth as he said it was up to me and I kept saying it is "your book" you need to tell me. And on it went.

Time flies during my visits with Father Claude. When I initially began visiting in the fall, I estimated I would stay about 30-45minutes. Well that never happened! Now it is almost 3 hours. I enjoy being with him, and I am not sure why I am so drawn to his company. We are actually having fun! We have singalongs, we dance and play trivia, it may be as simple as that. However, digging deeper I feel like he is the part of my family that is no longer with me. His roots are not far from my own town in Italy, and we now call each other cousins! He asks me to pray for him, and I ask the same in return. Who doesn't need more prayers? And I think he just might have a direct line to God and Saint Francis. He kisses and hugs me goodbye in typical, old school Italian fashion, and I do the same. Time, however, does not fly by on my return home! But the extra time in the car allows me to reflect on our visits. Could it be the stars aligning, Kismet, Divine intervention?

Il Volo's, song Capolavoro. Part of the (Chorus) lyrics are:

Io che mi sentivo perso, una vela in mare aperto
E all'improvviso tu, tu
Cadi dal cielo come un capolavoro
Prima di te non c'era niente di buono
E come se, tu fossi l'unica luce a dare un senso
E questa vita con te è un capolavoro

Translation
I felt lost, a sail on the open sea
And suddenly you, you
Fall from the sky like a masterpiece
Before you there was nothing good
And as if you were the only light that made sense
And this life with you is a masterpiece

As I ponder these lyrics, I realize that Father Claude has provided me with precious moments in my life's journey. My life has taken on new meaning while visiting this spiritual, no frills, humble, intelligent and gentle man. I hope I can be some Light to him. He has given so much to me.

Father Claude May 17, 2024

Fortunately, someone was available to help me with my heavy tote bag as I entered Father Claude's floor. Today was "a work on the book day", so I had to bring my laptop and my "A Game" to remember everything Father would tell me. He waved to me as I cautiously walked down the busy hallway balancing the pizza along with my bag. Amazingly, I made it without a mishap. He looked very handsome in his navy-blue polo shirt. I on the other hand looked like the bag lady that I indeed was.

"Peggy is the book done?" he asked. "Almost Father", I feigned. As I had told him it was a workday, he was very excited. We read through two chapters of the book and Father commented and I had to change some information I got wrong. As he hears what I have written, his recall is enhanced, and I get more information. A win, win.

He loved the pizza and the chocolate chip biscotti I brought. I felt a bit remiss because in my haste to get to Father Claude on time, I forgot his mandarin oranges and his olives. "Next week Father", I promised and "hopefully homemade meatballs". How silly, is there another kind I don't know about?

Father helped me clean up our lunch and I could tell he was tired, but he sat out in the corridor chatting with other residents. We kissed and hugged a couple of times to say "Good-Bye, see you next week". Baci e abbracci! Più tardi la prossima settimana.

Father Claude May 21, 2024

This is a very special day! Father's anniversary of his Ordination, (May 21, 1962), 63 years ago. I made him a special antipasto and meatballs and brought a baguette of crusty bread from Salumeria. He dug in hungrily, before I got all the food out on the table! Andy came to celebrate as well. We had extra sweet raspberries and juicy mandarins for dessert and finished off the meal with some decadent hazelnut cookies. This was another "work meeting" as it was the last visit to Father before the book went to the publisher. I did discover that Father can read very well in both Italian and English. His eyesight is very good as he reads with fluidity, and with intonation and cadence and that brought tears of joy to my eyes. Father complimented me on the translation from Italian to English, but I justly gave credit to Google Translate, although I do check their translations. I needed to get as much information as I could and Andy was certainly a huge help. We were able to get some answers where there were gaps in the timelines.

Soon the book would go to the Publisher. I knew from past experience that editing was, well, worse the ironing, my most dreaded chore. But Father is very excited! And that's all that matters. God Bless you! Dio ti benedica sempre.

Peggy Fucillo and Father June 2024

North End August 2021

Parishioners/Friends

Clergy

Padre Frederico Cinocca

Father Michael Della Penna OFM

Gathering of Franciscans

Dedication of the reopening of St. Leonard Church – May 2019

Cardinal Sean O'Malley OFM Cap (back) Father Antonio Nardoianni OFM and Father Claude OFM

With Father Robert Caprio OFM

Father Claude OFM

With Father Robert Caprio OFM at High School Reunion
photo courtesy of Arthur Sonny Lauretano

About The Author

Margaret (Peggy) Fucillo

I was born in Boston's North End on Fleet Street. My mother was born in Airola, Benevento, my father's family and all my uncles were born in Chiusano di San Domenico, Avellino.

I was the first woman of my generation to attend college. I am a graduate of Boston College earning a M.A. in Political Science/Constitutional Law and did post graduate work at Harvard University. I am fluent in Spanish and worked in Urban School Districts teaching newly arrived immigrants. Recently, I have been an adjunct faculty at North Shore Community College.

I am a member of the North End Historical Society and a Parishioner at Saint Leonard's Church in the North End.

My first adult book, **My North End Family Stories: La gioia e il dolore** was published in 2023. I have also had my stories published in the North End Historical Society Newsletter and the Post Gazette/North End.

The Polcari side of my family had known Father Claude's family since coming from Italy. My oldest cousin went to school with him. However, I have only known Father since I started attending Mass at Saint Leonard's ten years ago. He captured my heart immediately.

www.ingramcontent.com/pod-product-compliance
Lightning Source LLC
Chambersburg PA
CBHW070518090426
42735CB00012B/2830